Encounters

Francesca Remigi

Life Stories Collected on the Road

London

Dedication

To my mother Luisa, my aunt Ginetta and my Albanian family.

Contents

Acknowledgements

I'm grateful to my mum, to my aunt Ginetta, my cousins Elisa, Laura and Giovanni for having the faith in me to write this book.

Thanks to Vera Elezi, Rory, May Elezi and Brixhilda Gjyriqi my family in UK.

I'm grateful to my friend Gayathirry Krishnamoorthy that helped me with the editing of the book.

Thanks to my friends and colleagues Kasia Matoga, Alok Pradhan, Shanti Wisniewska and Emily Barnes for all their support.

Thanks to my line manager Nigel Triner and Robert Mansfield that offered me the opportunity to work for Jacobs.

My deepest thanks to all those I love so dearly who have supported me on this journey.

Introduction

*"Nel mezzo del cammin di nostra vita
mi ritrovai per una selva oscura
ché la diritta via era smarrita.
Ahi quanto a dir qual era è cosa dura
esta selva selvaggia e aspra e forte
che nel pensier rinova la paura!" (Dante Alighieri)*

In one of the most challenging periods of my life, the homeless represented a lifeline.

I was going through a complicated period at work and I had some misunderstanding with someone who had been for me as a family since I moved to England. Life simply happens and happens without asking our permission. Sometimes it finds us prepared, sometimes it lets us down and it is very easy to lose the point of the situation. At that time, I had lost faith in other human beings, I felt alone and phone calls with my Italian family and my friends were no longer enough.

The integration in a country with cultures and traditions completely different from mine was a difficult undertaking.

In fact, England has one of the most diverse Labor forces, both ethnically and religiously, in all of Europe. This means that being culturally aware is an essential part of life and work in the UK.

When I arrived here, I was optimistic and full of initiatives but not yet culturally aware. Our background has a strong influence on how we interpret and interact with the world around us. It imposes the way we behave within a cultural group and shapes our expectations when we are dealing with people from different cultural backgrounds.

Problems can arise when we use the rules of our culture to interpret others' behavior and when we fall prey to cultures, stereotypes and wrong perceptions. Although I had some success in the UK, I was not able to fully appreciate it and I focused only on the negative things.

I was often upset with God because I didn't have the perfect life.

For a period of time, I attended church but with no any results. All my prayers used to end with: *"God have you finished taking the piss out of me?"*.

The answers I was looking for came soon; spending time with homeless people gave me back my serenity.

I didn't have much to offer except a few coins, a hug and a chat.

The hours I spent with them and the life stories we shared gave me back all the things I thought I had lost.

I found God on the streets and I finally managed to make peace with myself. I want to share this experience with you, a long journey that has profoundly changed me.

I have collected the stories of these wonderful beings in this book with the hope that you will change your point of view, of the people on the street.

The homeless are people as we are and each of them deserves to be listened and helped with all of our available resources.

A lot of people think that it is *"their own choice" to* live on the streets, believe me, it is not a choice to live on the road, it is rather a consequence of wrong life choices.

Many of the people I met ended up on the streets due to problems related to alcoholism and drug abuse.

Most of my encounters took place in London and its surroundings.

The town where I live is cut by the railway line that leads to the City, time passes slowly, punctuated only by the arrival and departures of the trains and by the insistent chatter of commuters, especially early in the morning.

Right here, along the avenue of the station, I have met the most beautiful souls.

The City is the opposite, a place rich in entertainment and a crossroads of different cultures. However, there are two sides of the same coin, the daytime London, a destination for tourists and a place for business, and the London of the poor, brutally marginalized by the system.

While in the course of the day London is depopulated of all its workers and tourists, it gradually repopulates of homeless during the night hours.

As Charlie explained to me there are two types of homeless, those who live and sleep on the street and the *part-time* homeless, who despite experiencing difficult situations have accommodation where to find shelter.

The next time you meet a homeless on your way home, even if you are swallowed by your daily routine, find the time to stop even for a short time, take a deep breath and listen to his/her story. Strip off any doubt, cover your ears and start listening   with   your   heart.

Chapter One

Olga

I didn't meet Olga in UK but in Italy, she was the first homeless who opened a huge breach in my heart and that's why I decided to tell you about her story. I always remember her with great affection, and I won't hide that when I do some tears still run on my face.

Olga changed something inside me and since I met her. I just see other *"people"* like me sitting on the street, before I used to see human beings on the fringes of society that most other humans keep away with distrust and contempt.

At that time, I had just turned thirty and I was commuting between Zugliano, a small town located in the north of Italy, and Verona the third largest city in northeast Italy.

My employer gave me the permission to join ARPAV (Italian Environmental Agency for Veneto Region) as a volunteer attendee in acoustics once a week.

I fell in love with acoustics during my master's degree course and so my goal was to become an acoustician.

My first day of volunteering I arrived very early at the Verona Porta Nuova station, it was raining heavily and as usual I did not have my umbrella.

Despite the abundance of years, I have not yet lost this bad or good habit. I decided to spend some time inside the station hoping that it would stop raining. I was nervous and I couldn't stand the idea to have a free cold shower in the morning on the first day of work experience.

I was still sleepy, so I decided to get a coffee. Another bad habit that I have not yet completely lost is to leave the house without checking my wallet.

I opened it, full of hope, and as expected I found it sad and empty, there was only some cash for my return ticket. So, I started rummaging through my pockets and I found the five rolled-up euros that my mother had lovingly tucked into my jacket pocket without me noticing.

I unrolled them and with a big smile on my face I went towards the station coffee shop.

I noticed a female figure next to the entrance, sitting on the edge of a flower pot, she had gathered all her belongings around her as if they were precious objects in such a way that they would somehow remain dry.

I couldn't resist the curiosity to go and talk to her. She looked like seventy years old, although sometimes it's difficult to guess the age of a homeless, because of the weather exposure and the poor life conditions time leaves them many more marks on their face and body than it leaves to those who live a less complicated life. She wore a long blue pink-flowered shirt that concealed a worrying thinness.

She didn't wear shoes, her feet were bandaged with makeshift gauze and an old newspaper pages, her ankles were huge and looked like two marble trunks. She wore a purple turban on her head and two beautiful blue eyes that smiles on her face.

As I watched her, she engaged in a conversation with me, *"hey young lady ... why are you staring at me? Don't you like how I'm dressed today? You know... I was in a rush"* and she broke the inconvenient silence that had been created with a disruptive laugh. It was the typical laugh of a smoker, a mixture of weird sounds and cough. I was used to this kind of laugh since I was a child, being the daughter of an avid smoker.

I was very embarrassed, and I didn't know what to say, she noticed it and once again taking the fun out of me she came up with: *"young lady... let's break the ice... Can we drink a hot drink? What do you think?"* and smiling she added *"Today is on you, young lady, and tomorrow I will pay you back, deal?"*

I kept silent for a few more seconds and then I started to laugh, I was in a situation that I couldn't handle.

I took some courage and with a tremulous voice I said: *"What's your name? I never offer a drink to a stranger."*

"Young lady, I'm Olga" she replied, and she added, *"and you small thing... what's your name?"*

"My name is Francesca... at least that's what they made me believe so far," I replied with my dry Italian humour.

"Francis.... you have a very nice name, well now that we introduced each other could you please offer me a cappuccino? I'm very cold."

"Of course, Olga, wait for me here."

I ran into the coffee shop at a supersonic speed for the fear of not finding her there when I was back.

I went out the shop with two cappuccinos, one for her and one for me, I sat next to her on the edge of the flower pot and in silence we began to keep each other company.

Once I finished drinking the strangest cappuccino of my life, I greeted her and, in the meantime, it had also stopped to rain.

I felt strange but I was happy, and I run to the work place.

With Olga it had become an unmissable morning meeting, I used to meet her at the same place every time I commuted to Verona. I used to shout at her from platform one: *"Olga cappuccino????"*, *"Go young lady go. I'll wait for you here."*

As time went on, the trust grew, and she confided in me and told me how she ended up on the streets

Occasionally when I raised a few extra bucks, I used to buy her cigarettes. I wasn't a smoker at the time, but every time she opened the cigarettes, the first one was always for me.

"Take it, this is yours", she used to tell me, and I never had the courage to reply back that I was not a smoker.

I kept those cigarettes in my backpack for years inside a small metal box and every time I tidied up my things, looking at that box I would start crying. Olga was Ligurian, she came from Genoa and was married to a guy from Verona, *"my soul mate"* she used to add when she was talking about her husband. Every time she was talking about her loved Giovanni, she showed me the ring she still had on her finger and she used to add: *"He never left me, He is always with me"*.

They didn't have children although she mentioned that to me that she would like to be a mother, *"But life... young lady... sometimes doesn't give you what you need."*

They both had worked doing manual jobs, and when her husband died, she fell into a very bad depression. She started to drink and was unable to stop.

She quickly lost her job and gradually she lost her friends and the house she lived for rent. I asked her if she had ever turned to social services, I made that question on more than one occasion, but she never wanted to give me an answer.

We had our morning breakfast together for a few months.

When I told her that my internship would be over in a few days, she walked away from our flower pot in great haste.

I sat there waiting for her, I was sure that she would soon return back to me.

As I expected she came back with two cappuccinos and two brioches in her hands and she said, *"young lady, today I'm paying you back."*

I thanked her and I hugged her as strong as I could, knowing that maybe I wouldn't see her again.

Life is strange, to my big surprise I met Olga again when I started working in Venice. I ignored the fact that Olga often moved between Verona and Venice by train.

She used to take the first train in the morning from Verona to Venice and she often stopped at Padova. One day I asked her if she had any affections or friends in Padua, she smiled at me and she added: *"Of course young lady, I am devoted to St. Anthony and sometimes I go to him to pray for my sins".*

The Basilica of Saint Anthony of Padova is a Roman Catholic Church located in Veneto, dedicated to St Anthony.

Unfortunately, at that time there was no more time for our coffee, the biggest issue had become to argue with the train controllers so that they would not get her off from the train. Sometimes she even started smoking in the carriages, when they scolded her she used to shrug her shoulders and when they asked her for the ticket, she used to answer them with a big smile on her face: *"Come on, I don't need a ticket, I am a princess and you know princesses do not pay"*

Chapter Two

Roger e Barney

Roger, the first homeless that I met in England, went back to sleeping on the street just a few weeks ago.

Now it's late summer here, although calling it summer sounds a bit funny after growing up in a country where summer means something completely different.

I hadn't met him since early January.

Last time I spoke to him he had so many plans, on how to straighten his life, and when I saw him sleeping at the usual place, behind the station's green wall, I knew something had gone wrong.

I called him twice as he was still in a deep sleep *"Roger... Roger... hey you buddy... wake up "*.

He opened his eyes slowly and after few seconds he replied: *"Hey darling... here I'm, I'm back to hell."*

"What happened Roger? ... Are you okay? What are you doing here again?"

"Fran... it's a long story, I'd rather not say it, maybe in the next few days, ok?".

"Roger come on, don't be an asshole... how was York?... have you been there? Talk to me... come on".

"Fran... leave me alone for God sake.... my life is a mess."

"Ok, I let you sleep for now, we will talk later".

"Do you promise?".

"Ok, …see you later".

Roger is a fifty-six-year-old man, he is very tall, he has two very big hands, as a pianist my grandmother would say, and a long unkempt white beard that hides his cheeky smile.

He always wears a green baseball hat that leaves its place of honour on his head only to a grey wool one that he wear just before to go to sleep at the *"Mondo Hotel"*, as Roger says not just a few stars hotel, but a luxury one where on the most serene nights you can literally see the stars and count them all.

During the last winter he slept in the pedestrian tunnel that connects the centre of the town to the industrial area.

His house is a blue sleeping bag with two red stripes on both sides. Under the sleeping bag he uses a fold up cardboard to insulate him from the cold.

On the top of the sleeping bag he sewed a reflective band, in fact in that tunnel there are many cyclists sometimes oblivious to the nocturnal inhabitants lying there and as Roger says it's better to avoid being smashed on the ground.

On the other side of the tunnel there is a pub that allows him to wash himself in the morning when he gets up. Sometimes they also offer him something to eat and to drink.

The neighbourhood where I live is a neighbourhood of good people who help those in need.

Roger is a very skinny man and when he is tired, he bends heavily on his back holding on to his hips. When he does it, he smiles, and he swears that not long time ago over his hips there were two beautiful love handles. As an adult he lived in

Asia. Then he ended up in jail for a fraud he committed with Barney his partner in crime.

Barney is about Roger's age, he's got funny carrot-coloured hair that he says he inherited from his Irish grandfather. He worked for a long time in a chicken factory and as you can expect he hates chicken from the bottom of his heart.

He met Roger a few years ago and they immediately became best friends so much that they ended up even sharing the same space in jail.

After their detention they were deported to the UK and sadly the road has become their home.

Roger had asked for help to the government when he returned back to England, but he was not able to get back into the system and he had no family here to support him.

He certainly has some ex-wives scattered all around the planet.

He has been married almost three times. He admitted on several occasions that even when he is was perfectly sober; he was never a nice man and that he has deserved the escape of all his women, *"Fran my problem is not that I don't love women... I love all of them"*.

When he comes up with these statements, I always reply to him: *"Roger you should learn to love one woman at a time."*

The woman who left his heart empty and even his wallet was Ingrid his ex-German wife. The only one who apparently was able to stand to be with him. *"Fran...would you believe me if I told you that she was the only one I had ever cheated* on?", "of course Roger...". I have no idea if he has kids, and it always seemed inappropriate to ask him.

Barney, on the other hand, has an older sister and his mother, who he lovingly calls *"the old lady"*. His family have been trying hard to get him back home and he occasionally pleases them, in his own way, by camping with his friend Roger in their garden.

Neighbours usually stand the situation for a couple of days and then they complain about nocturnal shouting.

Roger told me about his childhood and his parents. He was apparently a happy child. His father was in the army and he had the opportunity to travel with him all around Europe. His parents passed away a few years ago and when he talks about them, he feels very guilty: *"I was never the son they deserved to have."*

Roger used to be a teacher, he lived a happy life until the craving for easy money took over.

He became a gambler and later an alcoholic.

Barney doesn't like to talk about his private life, he is more reserved, all I know is he was a troublesome young boy and has always been a difficult person. Unlike Roger, he doesn't seem to mind that much being homeless. He hates his sister and he often repeat that his parents have always loved her more than they loved him.

Also, never mention the word *"chicken"* if he is around or he will make some very weird reactions.

Roger likes to sing, and he also likes to play a small red harmonica. Only God knows how bad he is in music.

Singing however, relaxes him a lot, he says, and he makes fun of the bewildered faces of all those that listen to him.

14

One day he showed up at the tunnel with a traffic cone. Apparently, he had seen another guy using it as a trumpet and he decided to do the same. I'll let you imagine his brilliant results.

His favourite drink, unfortunately, is vodka that spills into the tunnel with Barney as soon as the light goes down. In England it is forbidden to drink alcohol on the streets and so they wait the darkness of the night, they hide in the tunnel and begin to drink like two fishes.

Sometimes in the morning they wake up with a black eye, in fact clouded by alcohol it happens that they fight for no reasons or for things that happened many years ago.

When you see Roger with a black eye, and you ask him *"why Roger? what did you do?'*, he tells you about Barney and smiling he points out that he's a big jerk. I've been inviting Roger to the pub for lunch a few times, and when you invite Roger, you're sure to find Barney magically appear soon after with one of his great stories.

I have some doubts on the truth of some of his stories, but I still listen to him, I keep quiet and if it is a funny story who cares if it really happened or it is a creation of his imagination.

The one that made me laugh more was the Hyde Park adventure, when they ran away with the vodka bottles that they stole from a Pakistani.

The Pakistani man "found" the vodka, who knows where, and once camped in hidden place at the park he started selling it to the other homeless at bargain prices. When Roger and Barney found out about the sale, they went to buy some bottles.

The Pakistani had to leave for a pee, and he asked Roger to look after the vodka bottles. Roger has a face of an angel and has a way to chat and stun anyone, but you shouldn't be fooled trusting him is a real gamble.

As soon as the Pakistani walked away Barney had the brilliant idea to steal the vodka. And so, they tucked as many bottles as possible into their pants and the rest in their backpacks and they ran away looking for liquor stores to resell the loot.

They ran a lot and in a clumsy way that they caught the attention of not only passers-by but also of two policemen who arrested them, and they got, as Roger said, *"a free night in jail"*. When they talk about it, Roger points out that it was Barney's fault and that they should have *"taken"* a couple of bottles to celebrate the lucky day.

Roger's plan for his future was to move to the north for a period, he still had some friends there that owed him favours. The last time I met him, he told me that all week he had pretended to be a street artist. He was sitting next to a real artist not far from Trafalgar Square. The artist was very talented, and he used to draw realistic pictures on the pavement using coloured chalks.

In a moment of distraction, Roger stole two coloured chalks from the artist.

Roger was sitting there all day waiting for the artist to go away from the drawings, once the artist went away, he pretended that the drawings were his own creation.

He used to make a few tweaks here and there casually and he invented stories for whoever was looking at *"his drawings"* about how he had learned to draw from his father when he was a kid.

You must consider that Roger for drawing is totally denied.

The morning he was supposed to leave for his new adventure I didn't see him lying down in the tunnel. I only hoped that his dream had come true. Unfortunately, though seven months later I found him sleeping in the same place.

He hasn't told me what happened yet, but sooner or later when I meet him again, I know he's going to tell me his story.

Chapter Three

Larry

Larry is in his fifties, he is very thin, and he is just over five feet tall, *"Larry you are a small thing "* I used to tell him.

He lives in his own world and to me it seems like a wonderful place to live.

I usually meet him early in the morning, around six o'clock when he starts his work shift, Larry is always cold and even in the middle of summer you'll find him wearing his loved green hoody.

He wears a large coat that is also green. Like Roger, Larry goes crazy for baseball caps.

Occasionally, I give him some caps; he wears them for a couple of days and then the new cap would promptly disappear to make room for his old green one.

He does not live on the street, but he takes care of all the people who sleep in the area.

During the winter, before starting his shift, he checks that the people sleeping in the area are in good conditions and do not freeze.

The winter temperature during the night drops a lot and if the homeless don't find an adequate shelter they are assured to freeze. Larry has called the ambulance for some homeless people on several occasions. In one of those occasions, I was there and while he was waiting for the arrival of the paramedics, he touched my heart by his comforting words to the people lying on the floor.

He often repeats that everyone deserves a second chance in life and that no one should ever be left alone.

He never talks too much about his private life and is rather shy about it.

I know he loves old movies, sometimes he acts some of the dialogues of his favourite films.

I don't enjoy watching old movies and the only one I'm able to recognize (...I think) is a dialogue taken from the *Godfather*, when Larry plays Franky's role. At the end of his play he always sings the melody of the soundtrack.

One thing I know for sure is that he takes care of homeless as much as he can. Larry told me that few years ago a gentleman who worked in a bank not far from the station helped one homeless person find a job. Every time he tells me about this story his eyes sparkle. I really suspect that he is talking about himself even though I've never had his confirmation.

It took me over a year to establish a dialogue with him and to gain some of his trust.

At the beginning he was very grumpy. I used to stop and greet him, but he ignored me, he just looked at me without speaking but I could read in his eyes, the anger: *"what do you want? Do I know you? Leave me alone"*.

His attitude made me very sad, but instead of giving up, I kept saying goodbye and talking to him even though he seemed to ignore me completely.

One morning when I really didn't expect it, he started a conversation.

I met him near a traffic light, and he came out with: " *it's really cold this morning ...isn't it"*, *"of course, it's cold"*, I replied, *"What do you expect? It is winter and this is the UK."* He started to laugh with my big surprise and asked me where I was coming from, *"try to guess ...".*

"Well, you have a very funny talk ... I would say ... France?"

"You are wrong my friend! You have one more guess to win a coffee".

He stared at me for a couple of minutes, looking at my Italian air force cap.

"You're Italian, aren't you?", He said, proud of himself sure he'd got it right.

"Good job, you have just won a coffee!" He shook my hand and he introduced himself: *"I am Larry but for you I am John, John Wein".*

"Okay John, I'm Francesca but you can call me Fran".

We went into a coffee shop near the train station. I ordered two coffees, but they only made me pay for one. *"Coffee is free for Larry", one* of the bartenders told me, and he added: *"He is a lovely man, in the mornings he always helps us to set up the tables and the chairs and he keeps the area very clean".*

You should know that Larry always hangs out with a broom, which he lovingly calls *"Peter"*, it is his imaginary horse and sometimes, when there are not many people around, he rides his broom on the station boulevard.

He knows many things about history and on our Saturday morning chats he does not fail to make comparisons with the current political situation and some events that took place in the past.

I'm not very knowledgeable on the subject and being a bit wary for nature so while he is talking and citing some facts that happened in the past, I quickly check my phone and to my surprise he is almost right.

He is an enthusiast about geography and if you find him in a good mood, he tells you about all the wonderful places he visited when he was younger.

Perhaps he has never really been there but the way he describes the places leaves me glued to the road until he finishes speaking.

If you are lucky and Jonathan also hangs out there you can also watch a duel of the old far West.

Jonathan is not homeless, he is a gentleman that is easy to meet around the station and the public library, I have no idea if he is a pensioner or if he is still working. I really enjoy the gags that he has in place with Larry.

When Larry sees Johnathan coming, he hides himself behind industrial bins that are placed not far from the station. When Johnathan is close enough to him Larry comes out screaming *"Geronimo"* as loud as he can.

And so, for a year now, the mornings are no longer the mornings unless I meet Larry and the others near the railroad.

At Christmas I asked Larry for a hug, he was very embarrassed, and he nervously replied making himself smaller between his shoulder: *"I usually take a bath on Wednesday if it's okay for you I will hug you tomorrow"*.

I waited the day after, and I gave him the massive hug that he deserved.

In the morning he waits for me next to the station and he starts his tobacco ritual: he takes off his work gloves, he puts them on his small cart, and he takes a small metal box from inside his jacket pocket.

The small cart is held together by an old elastic band.

He waits quietly for me to come closer to him and he break the silence with: *"a cigarette for John... baby ..."*.

"Yeah I got you" I reply to him, smiling. I give him a cigarette that he puts in the cart at light speed for the fear I would change my mind.

I don't want to talk about all his complaints when I buy the king size cigarettes that do not fit into his damn box. When it happens, he puts it in his trouser pocket, and he says: *"if I don't smash it before ... I will smoke it at lunchtime"*.

Before leaving him to his work I promptly ask him: *"and today ... Larry who are you?"*.

He raises his blue eyes to the sky, he thinks for a while and smiling back, he replies: *"Today, I 'm Bruce, Bruce Willis baby, have a nice day. "*

Chapter Four

Charlie

I first met Charlie last November, I was going to a construction site located in central London.

I was in a bad mood, I didn't want to go to site that day because it was particularly cold and I was complaining on the phone to my mother, the way I always do when something doesn't go the right way

I didn't like wearing my work jacket it is two sizes too large and is a shocking orange colour.

That huge jacket made me look like a big orange with a safety helmet.

Looking at my reflection in the shops windows I felt very ugly.

I used to go to that site location about once a week to check the noise and vibration equipment.

In that area there are many druggies and it is easy to stumble in some of their bivouacs especially early in the morning.

I met Charlie not far from the entrance to the construction yard.

He was sitting there without shoes and his teeth were chattering from the cold. He didn't look like a drug addict

, his hands and arms showed no signs of any type of injections.

He didn't smell of alcohol but of pain and loneliness, his face was carved by hunger. Charlie is a very young boy I guess he is not much older than twenty.

He did not have a jacket to cover himself, he did not have a blanket, only a very dirty yellow T-shirt and it was possible to count his ribs one by one while he was hard breathing.

I saw him and immediately my heart was broken. I immediately asked him if he was okay or if he wanted me to call him an ambulance.

I would have given him my work jacket to cover himself, but my jacket had my company logo on the back, I was a coward, I admit, I was afraid that I would get in trouble.

"I haven't lost my heart yet, I really can't leave you in these conditions" so I started looking for a Charity Shop, thankfully in this country there are many of them.

Charity Shops are places where people bring used items and clothes and potential buyers can buy them at a cheaper price than in traditional stores.

I went in and looked for a jacket and a pair of shoes, guessing his size.

I stopped at the Mc Donald's in front of the station and I bought him something to eat. I gave him the jacket and the shoes, which in total had cost me less than 15 pounds; he began to cry like a child. He hugged me as my brother used to do when we were kids.

I sat just next to him and I asked if he wanted to tell me how he ended up on the road, and he started to tell me his story.

Charlie is Irish, he is the second of four brothers, in Ireland he was a decorator and he used to work with his father and his brothers in the family business.

Charlie had other plans for his future, very different from what his parents expected from him.

His dream was to become a mechanic but when he tried to talk to his parents about his plans, he didn't get much support from them.

The father strongly disagreed on Charlie's plans, parents sometimes know how to be deaf to their children's requests.

It didn't make any sense to Charlies' father; there was a well-established job that allowed the whole family to live, why look for something else?

I still remember what a friend of mine told me chatting in front of a cup of coffee not a long time ago: *"Fran, let free your loved ones when they can't find themselves"*, and so Charlie's mother, who had fully understood his son's unhappiness, let him free to find his way.

His mother had to convince his husband to let him go and from what Charlie told me, it was not an easy task.

Charlie prepared his red suitcase and he finally left Ireland for his London adventures.

Once he arrived in London his plan was to get a job and start studying to be a mechanic.

He could perhaps have done it in Ireland too, but his desire to get away and prove everyone wrong had the upper hand.

He started off as a bartender apprentice in a coffee shop and things seemed to work for a while.

London is known to be a very expensive city and day by day Charlie began to accumulate debts that in a short time he was not able to repay back. Blinded by his pride, he did not ask anyone for help, not even his mother who would have welcomed him back home straight away.

The path that led him to be on the road was tortuous and much quicker than he expected.

For a while, he was hosted by friends at their home, but when he lost his job, he found himself completely alone.

I asked him several times *"why don't you go back to your family?"* and he always replied: *"I'm too ashamed, my father was right, I'm a looser"*.

Charlie explained to me the difference between a *"real"* homeless and a *"part-time"* one, both however still needs help.

He gave me a detailed list of all the fake homeless people who live in his area showing also a little bit of resentment, from his point of view it's a sort of unfair competition to find food.

"Fran, I really live on the street and these people arrive for their daily shift, but they have a house where they can go to sleep and wash themselves, and have you ever looked at their hands? They are not like me, they are clean". After few seconds he added: *"you know…. there are also bastards amongst poor people "*.

Our weekly chat became quickly a must, he used to talk about his week and his childhood in Ireland. He was a happy child even if his father sometimes scolded him because he used to dream with wide eyes.

He had a normal life, without any drama and had grown up in a nice environment.

His biggest problem was his pride, a sort of constant struggle with his ego that at some point seemed to have taken over.

About six months ago I changed my job and I was not able to go to see Charlie anymore on a weekly basis.

I didn't even have the time to say goodbye to him and thank him for all our chats.

I returned several times to that area at the beginning of June, but I have never met him again.

When I don't meet them in the area I always hope for the best. I hope from the bottom of my heart he has finally found the courage to return to his family.

Chapter Five

Richie

Richie is a twenty-six years old man, whom Charlie would refer to as a *"part-time"* homeless.

Richie in fact doesn't lives on the street, he wanders around the various stations and in the evening, he goes to sleep at his mother's house.

Few years ago, he was a skilled worker but unfortunately, he had an accident at work and suffered a serious spinal cord injury that led to his disability in walking.

He can no longer do his previous work he was previously doing, he takes a monthly allowance for his disability, but this is not enough for him to survive, so he rounds up asking alms to passers-by.

Before the accident he lived happily with his partner, they also have a four-year-old son.

The incident completely changed his life and the lives of his loved ones.

He gradually closed himself off from the other people. As he says, he became full of hatred following everything that happened to him, he pushed everyone away, including his partner.

The only relationships he managed to keep are the one with the mother that he calls his "rock" and the one with his son that his partner lets him visit a couple of times a week.

His partner left him with a glimmer of hope, *"find yourself and then come and get your life back"*.

Sometimes people need to be shaken to convince them to fight not for others but for themselves.

Richie does all his best to be a good father even though he feels very guilty for not being able to provide for his son's sustenance.

He keeps three photos in his empty wallet, one of his father, who passed away a few years ago, his partner and his son.

The first time I met him he was sitting on a carton not far from where I live and he was reading an Excel book, there were two other fiction books nearby.

He was clean and tidy, he wore a red and white checked shirt and a pair of torn jeans, round glasses resting on his nose, he wasn't the kind of homeless I have previously met on the street.

His beard was well groomed, and his hands were clean and in order, he looked more like an intellectual than a street boy.

I noticed he was sitting awkwardly his left leg was completely stiff and he had leaned under a backpack to keep it raised off the ground.

I was curious, and I asked what he was doing sitting there.

"I'm studying" he replied smiling, in a couple of weeks I will take my exam for a Word and Excel license.

Then, even more intrigued, I asked him why he was sitting there so uncomfortably and not in the town library which, is just five minutes away from there.

And that's how he made some space between the things he had placed on the floor and invited me to sit next to him to tell me his story.

"Come on, sit next to me", he said.

He didn't have to repeat it twice, I put down my backpack and I sat down next to him.

He held out his hand and he introduced himself: *"I am Richie"*.

"Nice to meet you Richie, I am Fran", he wanted to kiss my hand and I felt very uncomfortable, so I immediately stepped back.

I was a little dazed, he looked at me and said, *"Don't worry, I'm not crazy... it's that you look like my sister"*, I looked at him and we both burst out laughing.

I expected he was asking for money, but he didn't ask me anything, he just wanted to have a chat.

We agreed to see each other in the same place the next day, I brought him some fiction books that I had sitting at home.

We used to talk about everything as friends do when they meet for a chat.

People looked at us strangely, two people sitting on the floor drinking coffee and oblivious to what was going on around them.

One morning, one of the managers of the company I used to work for, who lives not far from my place, also passed by and when I arrived at the office, he heavily commented on my *"behaviour"* and that it did not suit the job role I held.

I was unable to hold back a big laugh that came out of my mouth quite naturally. I did not take the provocation, he had launched at me. I invited him to join us the next day at the same place and I didn't add anything else.

Sometimes the best thing it's to ignore provocations.

I learned it as an adult, but since I learned it, I laugh much more, and my gastritis has disappeared.

The funny thing is that manager accepted my invitation and the next day he presented himself with three takeaway coffees.

He did not have the courage to sit with us, but he remained there chatting for a while.

When we returned to the office he apologised and since then he has become one of the many homeless supporters in the area and I am sure that sooner or later I will see him sitting on the pavement.

Changes take time but a good start makes the job easier.

The morning meetings with Richie ran for a couple of weeks until he finally took his test.

His exam was on a Friday and I didn't see him for the whole week.

I was worried that something had gone wrong and not seeing him around my head was full of questions and bad thoughts.

Even though I hadn't known him for a long time, I truly wished he would pass his exam and stop being a part-time homeless.

When I finally met him a few weeks later he had a beautiful smile on his face, no cartoons at that day, he was resting on the station wall. It was the first time I saw him standing and the leg issue was even more noticeable.

He passed his test and thanks to his mother's friend he got an interview in a supermarket.

That day he invited me in the coffee shop next to the station and he offered me hot chocolate with cream, his favourite drink.

He told me he was grateful for the time I spent with him talking to him.

I thanked him for the same reason and for sharing his life experience with me.

Since then, I have never met him again, and in my heart, I really hope to never see him again on the road.

Chapter Six

Amir

I met Amir in a pub and not on the street and for a long time I was not aware that he was living right there.

It was Friday night and it was very busy week at work, so I decided to gratify myself with a beer.

At that time, I had some misunderstanding with my line manager and so I was marginalized by my team, things that sometimes happen due to incompatibility.

When my manager was around, my work colleagues would not invite me for a drink after work, perhaps because of the fear we would have an argument.

So, I found a pub not far from the office where there was no chance of bumping into him or my colleagues after working hours.

If a pub has hardly anyone there, there was a fundamental reason for it. The pub I had chosen to go to be such a sad place that even if you hadn't been upset, just going through the door would have catapulted you into a parallel dimension of deep dissatisfaction and melancholy. The lights were dimmed, the red carpet scattered everywhere and with no taste, it simply looked as a potential crime scene of any detective movie. The average age of the people sitting around was about fifty and even if a boy had entered the door *"puff"* he would have immediately turned into an old man with a stick.

There were no sofas, only old and dusty armchairs and their colour didn't fit the surrounding furniture.

I went straight to the bartender and I ordered a beer.

While I was waiting for my beer, I put the cigarette pack on the counter.

The bartender asked me: *"Do you want to smoke? the smoking area is down there beyond the toilets"*.

If in modern society smokers are a deeply despised category, in England they are even more, in fact they are very often relegated to areas that seem to be real places of punishment.

I grabbed my beer, I followed the cardboard arrow badly stuck to the wooden wall, I made a cross sign on my chest and I pushed the gate that led to the back.

There was only one red bulb light off a shed in a remote corner and light time button was being pressed in turn by other smokers.

I already imagined my place in the obituary and in my head, I could hear the echo of my mother's voice repeating to me *"you are a fool"*.

I put my beer on the small fence wall and lit a cigarette.

I noticed a gentleman standing alone, he looked very sad. He had two deep black eyes and his face was marked by time, between the wrinkles he wore on his forehead I saw the pain of a difficult life. He reminded me of someone, it seemed to me that I had already met him, but I just couldn't focus where and especially when it happened.

I introduced myself and we started talking. I asked him what was wrong with him and if he was a happy person.

I like to ask this question to everyone that I meet. This habit, started few years ago when I had depression, at that time I felt terribly wrong, I didn't have much support from my friends, they were too busy with their own life, and I often wished that someone found the time to ask me: *"How are you? Are you ok?"*.

"Yes", he replied without thinking too much, "*I am a happy man.*"
Amir is Algerian. His parents had some marital issues and so his father kidnapped him when he was still a kid and left him with his grandmother, who raised him.

Amir told me that his grandmother was a very strict person, and in more than one occasion she beat him up.

However, he was grateful to her because she had taught him discipline and respect for other people even if it was in a hard way.

His father had rarely visited him, after the divorce he had a new life and Amir was no longer any part of it.

He completed his philosophy studies in France thanks to the financial help of a wealthy aunt who had taken his situation to heart and after living in Belgium for some time he had moved to England.

He met his mother when he was an adult, but he did not have too much time to spend with her because she passed away just a couple of years later.

His mother, the mother that he had hated so much because he had been told that she had abandoned him, had never really stopped looking for him.

They remained in close contact as long as fate permitted it.

He impressed me for his way of thinking and the personal matters he was dealing with.

He had opened his heart to a stranger and told me about his whole life.

His speech didn't catch only my attention, other smokers came to listen to his story.

Without realising it, we found ourselves in the middle of a life lesson.

He explained that to be happy he had fought for a long time against his immense ego but at the end of the story his commitment and perseverance helped him to dominate his fears

He then began to talk to us about some philosophers who inspired him and who had somehow show him the way forward.

That was how we became his Friday nights' students.

He had the ability to make interesting subjects that for me had always been difficult and I had never appreciated and did not completely understood when I was at school.

We used to ask him a lot of questions and he seemed very happy for the interest we were showing him. I still remember his wonderful speech about Plato.

We met there every Friday night for about six months and none of us ever missed the weekly appointment.

Then suddenly Amir disappeared, no one heard from him for months.

We wondered where he was, we missed his lessons a lot and we were worried that something bad had happened to him.

I went to the pub for another couple of months, still hoping to meet him again, and then I stopped going there when I changed my job.

Life never stops to surprise me, when I came back from my summer holiday, one morning I received a beautiful and unexpected gift.

I was waiting at the train platform and not far from me there was Amir.

I ran to him and hugged him tightly, *"Amir, how are you?"*.

He smiled and replied: *"I am fine thanks and you?"*.

We went out to the station to get a coffee and we talked a lot.

He told me that when we first met him, he was still living on the street, the job he told us about was not real, although to be honest he had never given us too many details about it.

Amir had lost his job. He had other plans for his life, he wanted to be a teacher, but he ended up on the shelves of a supermarket to pay his bills.

The dissatisfaction for not having realized his dreams and his finance issues pushed him to alcoholism.

After several arguments with his wife who was trying to help him, he ended up on the road.

After a long period of confusion, he decided to return to his wife and put himself in rehab.

His partner who loves him deeply welcomed him home again.

Amir got help and was detoxified from alcohol.

After working long and hard on himself he managed to find another
job and he finally started to live life again

Chapter Seven

Cindy

I met Cindy during a night-time acoustic survey.

I have always hated the night shifts alone, both for the cold and for the fear of finding some bad guy on my way.

I used to walk with a pepper spray, that I bought on amazon, in my backpack with the conviction that it would protect me from everything, as soon as the measurement position was set and the instrument calibrated, I used to transfer my defence weapon inside my jacket pocket and I felt like a superhero

The areas that I detested more were those of the City, in fact during the night the office areas become depopulated making the nocturnal inhabitants slowly come out.

During the day, London is a beautiful city and sometimes I get excited as I walk through the streets and admire its architecture, buildings of all kinds and shapes but at night it seems to be swallowed in one bite.

The poor lighting makes everything gloomier, and even a little mouse that runs oblivious on the street seems to you a potential mutant that will soon turn into something scary.

If you have a vivid imagination ... you can see werewolves, witches and vampires at every corner. My supervisor that day called me in his office just before the end of the work day for a measurement that had to be taken urgently, my colleague was sick, and I was told someone needed to do the job.

"When?", I asked him a little bit annoyed.

"Early morning", he replied, smiling.

"Early morning? When? and at what time?", I replied.

The *"early morning"* strategy consisted in sending you out to take measurements in the middle of the night but without paying you the night shift.

The trick was to add that *"early morning"* between the paperwork and "puff" the extras of the shift dissolved in a beat of wings.

"Two o 'clock", he added with a cough.

My boss used to cough when he was nervous.

I returned home, with just enough time to eat, take a shower and leave for my measurements.

I arrived on time at the established place, I looked around and as expected there was not a living soul.

I set up my tripod and began to prepare the instrument, I was absorbed in my thoughts and when I looked up, I found myself facing a human presence.

"What is that? Are you a journalist? Are you doing a service?", she asked me all in one breath.

"No, I'm not a journalist, I'm an engineer and I'm involved in an acoustic survey"

"Acoustics?"

I gave to her a very boring explanation on acoustics science.

While I was talking to her, her eyes lost more and more interest and at a certain point I felt so sorry for her that I stopped my acoustics lesson. I had responded to her curiosities, it didn't matter if I had stunned her with technical terms and legal limits, after all she asked for that, so I felt entitled to be able to ask her something too.

I introduced myself and I asked her to do the same.

She told me her name was Cindy and she was Romanian, I remained silent for a few seconds and then I exploded in a loud laugh.

She looked at me astonished and then she asked me what I found so funny...

"Romanian? Cindy? Come on buddy tell me your real name".

"Michaela", she added straight away.

From experience I can state how much easier it is to tell the truth to perfect strangers than to our own family and friends.

Michaela was over thirty, she was very thin, and she had two very sad eyes.

She had arrived in England with what she thought was her boyfriend but who immediately proved to be an exploiter after her arrival, he sent her to prostitute herself on the streets.

She had very different dreams when she came from Romania, but she found herself living a life of violence and abuse.

She still had her family in Romania, but she was very ashamed of being a prostitute and she didn't have the courage to go back home.

"I'd not be able to look at my mother's eyes", she told me.

Her parents weren't very happy that she was leaving Romania, but they finally were convinced, and they trusted the promises made by what looked like a good man. She kept in touch with her family for a while, pretending that everything was fine, masking her situation with so many lies.

When she could no longer lie to her family, she did not choose to tell them the truth she preferred to disappear for the fear of being judged.

In my backpack I had a thermos of coffee and my packet of cigarettes, so we drank a cup of coffee and we smoked a few cigarettes. We sat together on a low red wall not far from the instrument and we had a little chat before I started my shift and then she walked away.

She didn't ask me for any type of help.

At the end of my shift I started collecting my things and with my surprise she come back to me to say goodbye, I thanked her for our chat, and we greeted each other with a hug.

Since then I have not met her, but I still remember her last words: *"find another job and stay away from the streets especially during the night, the streets can be much more dangerous than you think"*.

I treasured her words and a few days later I had a long chat with my manager because I didn't feel secure to go on night surveys by myself.

At the beginning of the conversation when I told him about my concerns, he was a little bit angry, as I expected, but at the end of our meeting he was supportive.

Not more than a week later he put in place a new procedure to send at least two people for night shifts.

Chapter Eight

Joe

Joe is a very young man in his twenties, and I often happen to see him sleeping on the streets of the town.

For most of his time he is drunk, and he lies down unconscious on the ground.

He usually wears a red jerky suit and a very light brown jacket that is a bit tight.

 He stinks of every type of alcohol and chemicals and for this reason sometimes it is difficult to stand next to him.

When he is awake, he tries to accumulate enough money to buy drinks.

He is usually standing near the local pubs where he has no shyness in asking customers to take him with them and offer him a 'round' or sit in front of the supermarkets with the hope that someone will buy him something to eat.

He is the only homeless who ever asked me for money and the only one that offered to buy me drugs. At that point I realised that maybe he was involved in some drug dealing.

I have always limited myself to offering him only a few cigarettes and some sandwiches aware of the fact that he does not use the money to eat but to get drunk. His gaze is lost in the nowhere, and he seems to live in a sort of parallel dimension, it is almost impossible to enter his world.

I have tried several times to engage in conversation with him, but I always end up with very disappointing results.

He doesn't like talking about himself, he just asks you for money, nothing else.

One day I asked him how he got into alcoholism and what made him start drinking.

He candidly replied that he simply likes to do it. Unlike other people with alcohol problems that I have chatted too, he is the only one who has not told me about a difficult life or personal issues that have become unsolvable.

Some of them told me they were drinking to stun themselves and not to think about their daily problems, others told me that they started out as casual drinkers and quickly found themselves in habitual ones.

Joe has not tried to give any justification for his personal situation; he just told me that he does it because he likes it.

I asked him if he ever thought to stop drinking, the answer I received was not very different from the one he had repeatedly expressed in our previous conversations: *"I like to drink and I'm fine with that"*.

His disarming answers have not given space to any kind of dialogue, it is like talking to a wall. Wrapping up your thoughts and questions in a big ball and you launch it to him, hoping he starts to play, but shortly thereafter the ball comes back to your face. After having recovered from a ball straight in the face that you have deliberately asked for, you raise your gaze to the sky in a daze and you can see all your questions floating in the air waiting for the wind to take them far away. I discovered his good heart on a February day. I came back tired after a demanding shift; I couldn't wait to get home, to eat something and quickly go to sleep. When I got off the train, my head began to turn, I hurried to the stumbling exit. I fainted from tiredness and find myself lying on the ground. When I recovered, next to me there was Joe holding my hand. He was scared and crying.

"Why are you crying? I feel better now ", he looked at me and he replied: *"I was afraid that you would not wake up again"*, and he asked me if he could hug me.

I had allowed myself to judge him and I had done it so badly, that hug had more value for me than all the words he had never told me before and his story that he had never wanted to share with me.

I'd like Joe to get help, it's never too late to start again, but until he realises that alcohol is his worst enemy, he'll be locked up in the cage he has built for himself.

Chapter Ten

Fran

In a summer evening, not long time ago, I was sitting in the garden, I wondered what I learned from all these experiences, and I finally found some answers to my queries.

I learnt to never judge other people by appearances.

I learnt how alcohol and drugs can be destructive.

I understood what it meant to be hungry and I realised how much food I was wasting.

I understood what it means to be cold and the importance of having a jacket to cover yourself.

I learnt that it is important to take care of the others.

I understood the meaning of forgiveness; how much we suffer when we are not granted by others and how much we suffer when we are not able to forgive ourselves.

I tried to live without God, and I realised how important it is to believe in something.

I have more questions and maybe I will find the answers that I am looking for once again on the street.

Francesca Remigi was born in Malo (VI) Italy and she lives in London since 2013. She is a civil engineer and she holds a PhD in Industrial Engineering. She currently works between Croydon and London dealing with noise pollution. In her spare time, she likes reading books and writing. In 2009 he published *"Oblio"* her first collection of poems and in 2012 *"Ragnatele"* another collection of poems.

www.ingramcontent.com/pod-product-compliance
Lightning Source LLC
Chambersburg PA
CBHW051125250726
48655CB00007B/2897